I CLIMBED

A RAI... ...E

by Christopher A. Lane
illustrated by Stephanie Britt

THE C. R. GIBSON COMPANY
NORWALK, CT 06856

Text copyright © MCMXCIII Alpha-Omega Productions
Art copyright © MCMXCIII Stephanie Britt
Published by The C. R. Gibson Company, Norwalk, CT 06856
ISBN 0-8378-5304-4
GB365

I climbed a rainbow once.
Can you guess what I found?
A shower of bright colors
Reaching from the ground.

I shall not forget the sight,
It was a wonder to behold,
But a story of this nature
From the beginning should be told

I donned a new kerchief,
And took up my picnic sack
In case I saw an angel,
Or hungered for a snack.

I then began my journey
Climbing up into the sky,
So I could reach the top
Before the sun was high.

I climbed and climbed the rainbow,
Never looking down,
And as I walked its colored path,
I didn't hear a sound.

The air was still and quiet
Like my room before the dawn.
I began to worry
That my folks would find me gone.

So I hurriedly went skyward
My wonder ever growing.
What would I find at rainbow's end?
My curiosity was showing.

The clouds were down below me,
Puffy, pink and white.
They looked like misty marshmallows
Dancing in the light.

There were no birds about
For they soared down below.
I saw no kites or aeroplanes,
It was too high for them to go.

When I reached the top
I paused to breathe a sigh,
And then I felt a shiver,
Though I'm not sure just why.

Perhaps it was the chilly air,
Perhaps it was the height,
Perhaps it was the stunning view,
The beauty of the sight.

For far below, beneath my feet,
The land was stretched out flat.
There were farms and towns
Just scattered like patches on a mat.

I thought I saw some people,
They looked like tiny ants.
They were moving in all directions,
Some in circles like a dance.

0008850

9582 c-2

0008850 9582

Sell your books at
World of Books!
Go to sell.worldofbooks.com
and get an instant price
quote. We even pay the
shipping - see what your old
books are worth today!

Sell your books at
World of Books!
Go to sell.worldofbooks.com
and get an instant price
quote. We even pay the
shipping - see what your old
books are worth today!

Inspected By: Rafael_Ramos

0088509582

9582

00088509

c-2

S-5

The time came to go back down,
I pulled the hat from off my head,
And sat down upon it gently
To use it for a sled.

At first I didn't budge.
But then I gave a push
And moments afterwards
I took off with a swoosh.

I moved at such a speed
That my heart began to race.
I had never traveled
At such a thrilling pace.

I rushed just like a rocket
Down the shining bow.
How would I ever stop myself?
I really didn't know.

So I reached for my kerchief
And held it in the air,
Using it like a parachute
I yelled, "Watch out down there!"

It slowed me down enough
That when my feet touched down,
Instead of landing with a crash,
I simply plopped onto the ground.

It was such a wild ride,
A novel kind of pleasure.
But at this rainbow's furthest end,
I was looking for a treasure.

I'd heard tales of pots of gold,
And leprechauns in green,
But though I looked most carefully,
They were nowhere to be seen.

What I found that day,
At the end of the colored bow,
Was a note on palest parchment
In faded indigo.

"I am The Rainbow Maker,"
The letter started out,
"And I made you as well,
Of that there is no doubt.

"If you have come for riches,
Then riches you have found,
For I created all you've seen,
My wealth is all around."

At the bottom of the note,
The signature was odd.
It said, "I love you, faithfully,"
And the name below was "GOD."

When I began my journey,
To climb upon the arc,
I had done it playfully
As if it were a lark.

I learned something precious,
I didn't know before,
That He who made the rainbow
Will love me evermore.